Handbook of Infantry Tactics
for Paintball II, Urban Ops

Indoor and Urban operations specialized
warfare adapted for Paintball, Air-soft and
Laser-tag, MOUT, SWAT

www.InfantryTacticsForPaintball.com
www.TacticsForPaintball.com

ISBN: 1-4392-2811-6

Dedicated to my wife, step daughter, son and all of those who've served honorably in any branch of the United States Military.

E co. 1/41 Inf. 2 AD
HHC 2 Bde. 2 AD
C co. 1/5 Inf. 2 ID (Korea)
C co. 1/9 Cav. 1 Cav.
C co.1/108 Inf 27 ID (NY)
D co. 2/108 Inf 27 ID (NY)

Table of Contents

The terms man, him, he, etc may be used for either gender.

Preface

This book covers the basic fundamentals of urban warfare adapted for combat sports. The techniques illustrated are based on military MOUT and SWAT training.

In a real world combat environment, taking a city from an organized and competent military force, such as in WWII, 30-40% casualties were expected, assuming also that the odds are in your favor as an assaulting force of at least a 3 to 1 ratio with air and artillery support. Basically, it takes 3 men to take out 1 man defending an urban area and 2 will walk out battered but hopefully relatively unscathed.

This book is a primer or refresher of urban combat skills adapted for paintball, laser-tag and air-soft. Some methods have been modified for the game.

Enjoy and play safe.

Safety:

- Always point your weapon in a safe direction or at the ground.

- Never point your weapon at anything unless you intend to destroy or paint it.

- Always follow the range or course rules and guidelines for Safe and Fair play.

- Follow the manufactures recommendations for your particular weapon.

1. Basic marksmanship:

1.1 Sights:

Become familiar with the sights on your particular weapon. It's fun to 'fire from the hip' or to pretend to be some 'cowboy gunslinger' or 'gangsta', but accuracy leads to winning. A single accurate shot is much more effective and a lot more fun than a whole container of 'full-auto' missed shots.

Most paintball guns don't have functional sights or aren't very accurate using the fixed sights combined with the ball container (hopper) on top of the weapon where the sights should be. The paintballs themselves are often out of round or almost elliptical. For these reasons, reliable accuracy will be very difficult to obtain. Fire a few practice shots to get a general idea of where your paintballs are going to land

and adjust from there.   Practice is always important.

A typical off the shelf paintball gun. Note the lack of sights.

1.2 Sight Picture:

The correct sight picture will have the tip of the front sight pin in the center of the rear peep sight hole (generally located on the top rear of the receiver) or the front sight pin will be flush (flat) along the top of the rear sight 'v' groove.   For further explanation, see your particular weapons owners' manual.

Breathing actually affects your shot. The rise and fall of your chest slightly changes the orientation of your weapon just enough to make you miss your target. Exhale before firing or just hold your breath, aim and fire.

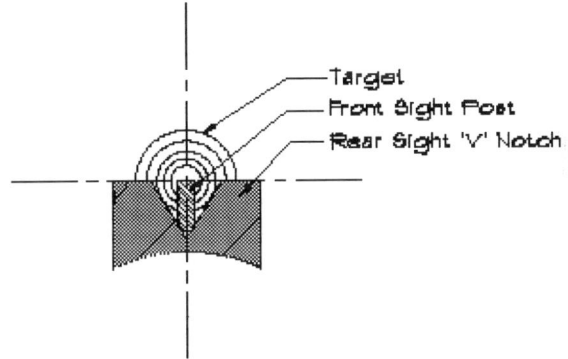

A typical 'V' notch sight

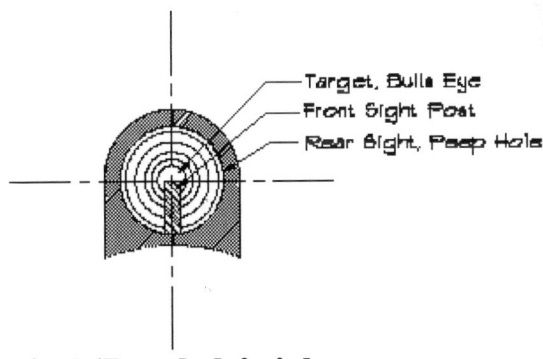

Typical 'Peephole' sight

1.3   Zeroing your weapon:

The best strategy is to zero your paint ball gun at 15-25 meters.

Fire three rounds into a target ranging from 15 meters to 25 meters away to find where your paint balls will land.   Adjust your point of aim (compensate) to hit the target or adjust your sights (recommended). Refer to your owner's manual for your particular model and follow the manufacturers recommendations on adjusting your front and rear sights.

Do not compensate (Kentucky windage) while adjusting your sights.   A small mechanical correction may be all you need.

Always use the same point of aim while attempting to 'Zero' your paintball gun.

Use three rounds at a time for each sight correction and practice your marksmanship for a tight group of shots to ensure that your rounds will fall on target and eliminate your opponent from play.

A paintball gun with accuracy will be a challenge to all that oppose your team.

Many things may cause your paintball gun to lose it's zero.   Bumping your weapon, dropping it, low Co2, playing with the sights...   They can normally be brought back, by re-zeroing your weapon.

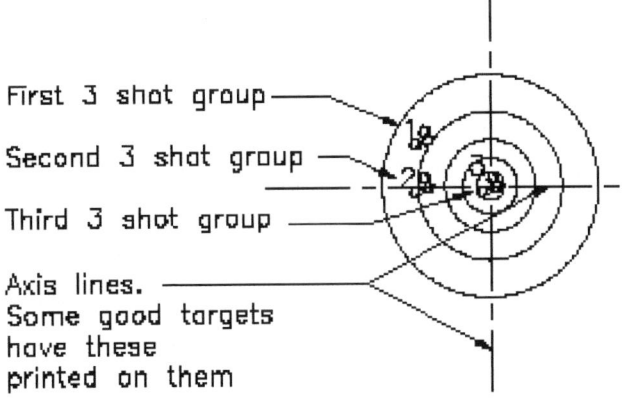

First 3 shot group

Second 3 shot group

Third 3 shot group

Axis lines.
Some good targets
have these
printed on them

Adjustable Front and Rear sights:

1. Fire a 3 shot group using the center of the bulls eye as your point of aim.
Bring your shot group down, first to align on axis with the bulls eye, using your oringinal point of aim.

2. Adjust front sight post per manufacturers recomendations up/down.
Generally raising the front sight post drops the shot group, Lowering it raises your group.

3. Fire your second three shot group.
Adjust your rear sights.
Generally, moving it to the right will bring the group to the left. Moving it left will bring your group to the right.

You should be on target. Repeat your 3 shot groups and adjust only your front or rear sights between groups.

Fixed Front and Adjustable Rear sights:

1. Fire a 3 shot group using the center of
the bulls eye as your point of aim.
Bring your shot group down, first to align on
axis with the bulls eye, using your oringinal
point of aim.

2. Adjust rear sight up/down per
manufacturers recomendations.
Generally, raising the rear sight post Raises
the shot group, Lowering it drops your
group. (Note) Raising your rear sight also
helps to fire from a distance.

3. Fire your second three shot group.
Adjust your rear sights side to side.
Generally, moving it to the right will bring
the group to the left.   Moving it left will
bring your group to the right.

You should be on target.   Repeat your 3
shot groups and adjust only up/down or
side to side between groups.

For weapons without sights, practice firing at objects at different ranges to determine how much the paintball drops during distant flight and what kind of spread the shots will have. Two shots using the same point of aim could land a few feet apart at a distance. Practice, Practice, Practice.

1.4 Marksmanship:

Practice your marksmanship and drop those rounds where you want them to fall. No more relying on luck and a ton of wasted shots... Good marksmanship comes with patience, practice, and a huge container of paintballs...

Zero your weapon, practice the fundamentals of marksmanship and shoot with confidence that you'll hit what you're aiming for. As the US Army Snipers say, "One shot, one kill.

1.5 'Kentucky windage':

Pick a point of aim at a tree or other object 20 feet or so away for a paintball gun, squeeze off a few shots and look at the difference between where you were aiming and where they landed. Then adjust your point of aim to where you think the paintballs will land.

For shots that a farther away, apply the principles of 'Kentucky windage' while simply aiming slightly higher to allow the paintball to arc until it makes contact with your opponents face shield.

Practice with a distant target, tree or opponent.

Chapter 1 Notes

2. Individual firing positions:

Individual firing positions are 'reflex' positions for our combat arms soldiers, namely Infantry. (Nothing against Armor or Artillery). These combat skills are adapted for gaming but the intent is the same. To quickly position yourself by reflex into a comfortable and steady firing position oriented towards your opponent.

These should be learned and practiced and are some of the most basic fundamentals to any combat engagement.

Even a seasoned veteran with actual combat experience is always practicing the most basic of techniques. Both on the rifle range and in the field, even after it has become a reflex the need to stay sharp is constant. Don't be afraid to get dirty!

2.1 Prone supported firing position:

Laying down ankles flat on the ground with your toes out, firing side knee bent. Support your weight with your elbows while resting your weapon on a sandbag, log or anything that holds your weapon in a comfortable position. Hold your cheek against the stock while looking down the sights.

It is difficult to hit someone who is lying down in the prone position. The effective target area is basically just your head and shoulders (from a distance), but that advantage is gone if they're right in front or above you. Combined with the fact that they may not expect you to be lying down, this position could be very effective, provided you have room to maneuver. But, even in close quarters paint-ball, a hit to the foot is still a hit.

Unconventional, but laying on your back may also be a very effective strategy for a close quarters one person hasty ambush, as long as you can quickly get up to change your position so that your opponent(s) cannot easily get your location or that you can effectively cover all avenues of approach. That would provide you with a new very painful hit location on your opponent.

You won't make many friends playing that way though.

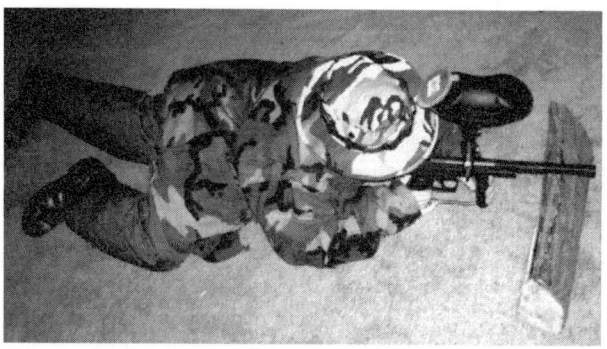

2.2 Prone unsupported firing position:

Laying down ankles flat on the ground with your toes out, Firing side knee bent. Support your weight with your elbows holding your weapon at a comfortable position. Use your bones, not your muscles to steady your weapon. Hold your cheek against the stock while looking down the sights.

2.3 Kneeling Firing Position:

(Right handed firer) right knee down with toes flat on the ground and sitting on your right heel. Left elbow rests on left knee while steadying yourself and aiming your weapon.

Kneel to reduce your profile and effectively make yourself a smaller target when occupying a defensive position. Kneeling allows you to quickly react to opponents behind you and also the ability to quickly get up and move.

2.4 Standing Firing Position:

Stand with your legs comfortably apart and facing the enemy. You can minimize your profile by standing with your non-firing side shoulder facing your opponent, with your weapon raised, looking down your sights or across the top or side of your weapon.

Weapon (at the ready)

Keep your weapon raised, to your cheek, ready to fire.   Wherever you look, your weapon should follow.   The same principles as our attack helicopters chain guns.

Quick reflexes and reaction are the only things that will keep you in the game. With your weapon already up and ready, if you see an opponent, all you have to do is squeeze the trigger and your opponent is out of the game.

2.5   Walking firing position:

Walking with weapon "at the ready", Raise weapon to align the sights with your target.   Bend knees slightly and take slow 'sure' steps, heel to toe. Reflex (Aim-point type) sights are recommended to improve accuracy.

2.6   Close Assault, Running while firing (for suppression):

Running with weapon raised, sights aligned with target. (Good luck on hitting anything at a distance).   Good for enemy suppression while assaulting the objective.

If you are running to change positions, withdraw or whatever, Always run in a straight line. Zigzagging doesn't work and makes you look like an idiot.

Bounding or rushing is the fastest way to move from one position to another. As a general rule, each bounding movement should last from 3 to 5 seconds. Another name for this movement technique is the **'Three to Five second Rush'** for a reason.

Try to keep rushes short to prevent the enemy from tracking you.

Always try to bound or rush from one place of cover to another.

Never bound into the open and extend your rush should you need to reach cover. The longer you are exposed, the easier it is to hit you.

Chapter 2 Notes:

3. Personal & Team Posture

The best trained and disciplined individual can only be one small part of a team.   One person that knows what they are doing isn't going to be able to help everyone else.   Ensure that each team member knows by reflex what to do when the paintballs are flying.

Reflex learning is obtained by doing the same thing over and over until it's a 'reflex'.   Learn your basic individual and team posture by practicing as a team.

Go through your battle drills beginning with the crawl phase, walk phase and run phase.

Crawl phase: Each person in the team practices their individual movement techniques, posture, and each position in the basic 4 man stack.

Walk phase: The team gets into the 4 man stack and walks through clearing a room or building. Rotate positions so that each man can perform each job in each position.

Run phase: Your team moves through a building at combat speed. Violence of action is key. Keep your forward momentum going until the building is clear.

I haven't seen a single movie where they clear an entire building the way it should be done. One room at a time, Think 10 seconds per room. Quick decisions, violence of action, violent forward momentum, and one room at a time until the building is clear.

3.1 Stance, Facing the enemy

In an actual combat situation, wearing your body armor and other protective equipment, you have to be ready to absorb a hit from a rifle or a blast from grenade or other explosive device and an armed enemy who wants nothing more than to take you with him. Typically the armored plates are in the front and back of your body armor and this is where you'd hope that, if you did get hit that's where it would go. The proper stance is facing the enemy, feet solidly planted, almost like bracing yourself for what would be an unexpected explosion of violence.

In paintball, you don't have any of those concerns. Stand comfortably while trying to minimize your exposure and target profile. Turn sideways to make yourself a smaller target. You do have to worry about the unexpected violence, but without the life taking consequences.

Note the posture of the person in this picture. Shoulders square with his target, feet comfortably apart and almost bracing for impact.

For paintball though, he is unnecessarily exposing his entire front profile to incoming paintballs.

3.2 Basic 4 Man Stack

The traditional swat team stack is perfect for storming a room and going against real bullets and quickly overpowering the enemy, but in paintball or laser-tag, your opponent may not stop firing when they get hit. Because of this, it makes sense to spread out a little until you are just about to enter the room. It is not advised to travel or move in this formation during game play, but it may offer some advantages.

The 4 man stack allows your entire team to go through a choke point (door etc.) almost all at once to overpower a defending opponent.

If you move in a stack formation you can use your fallen comrades as human shields for the first burst of fire from your opponent, but that is not advised, and I'd hate to be on your team.

The 4 man stack may be expanded to allow a 5th or 6th member.

The first man stands facing forward down the hallway, with his weapon in the ready position.

The second man stands just behind the first man, holding onto his shoulder with his free hand and holding his weapon to the ready around the side of the first mans head.

The Third man stands behind the second man, again holding onto his shoulder with his free hand or pushing his elbow into the second mans back, and keeping his weapon at the ready to cover the formations side or flank.

The Fourth or last man provides rear security, so that no one comes up behind the formation. The fourth man stands as close as possible to the third man so that he knows when the formation moves without speaking.

He should be the only member without physical contact with the other team members while moving and will regain contact when the formation stops, normally by bumping into the guy in front of him (behind him because he's facing backwards).

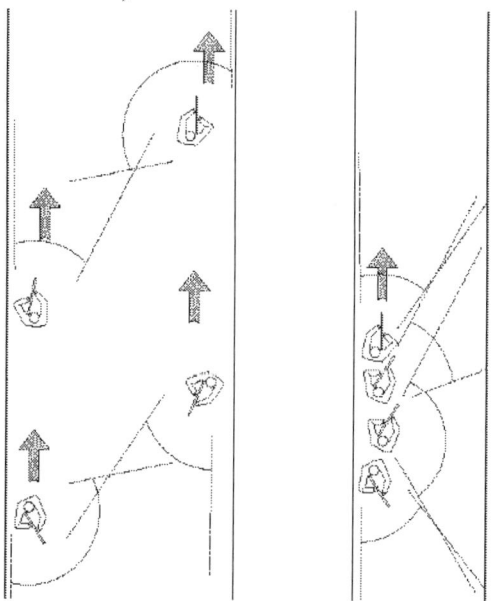

3.3 Individual Sector of Fire:

Your individual sector of fire is generally straight ahead or an orientation assigned to you. Left flank, Right flank, Rear security. Prevent a "friendly" from entering your sector of fire by adjusting your sector to the left or right.

In a defensive position your sector of fire is straight ahead and 45 degrees to the left and right (90 degrees in front of you). The sectors of fire of the fighting positions next to you on either side should overlap yours.

While moving, your sector of fire will be what is assigned, while slowly scanning from the front (to see where you're going), side (predetermined left or right) and rear. Or to your front and each side in a sweeping motion, if you're leading the element, ensure that the rest of the team trailing you is covering the sides and rear.

You are scanning your sector of fire while moving. Your lead element may pass a hidden opponent. It is every team members' responsibility to scan to form an effective perimeter. Don't just follow the leader until your face shield turns red. The whole idea is for you to see them before you get in their kill zone. Otherwise just study how to get yourself out of a close ambush.

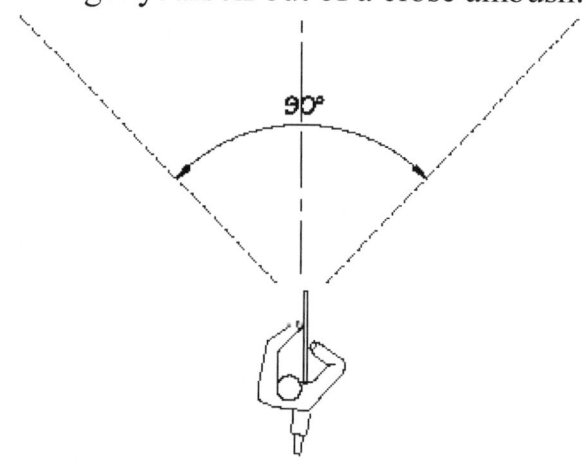

3.4 Team Sector of Fire:

Each individual in a team, moving in any formation should be pre-assigned a sector of fire.   Scanning their respective sectors, each individual should be scanning for their next position or cover, and signs of the enemy.

While scanning your particular sector of fire be sure to employ the principles of moving with stealth.

Ensure that 360 degree security is established because the enemy could have snipers or observation posts out that could easily be in a position to flank you. Looking behind you every once in a while could prevent them from winning.

Overlap your sectors of fire, and do not allow any of your team mates into your sector of fire, and do not move into someone else's sector of fire.   You are keeping them from rapidly reacting to enemy fire.

Generally your sector of fire is 90 degrees in front of you, if you are the first man, or leading a column.

Your sector of fire is either assigned or according to your position within the team.   Generally speaking it is straight ahead or 90 degrees to your right or left, opposite from the person in front of you if in a column.

If you are the last man, rear security would be your responsibility.   Prevent your team from getting flanked or a hidden opponent behind from wiping out your entire team.

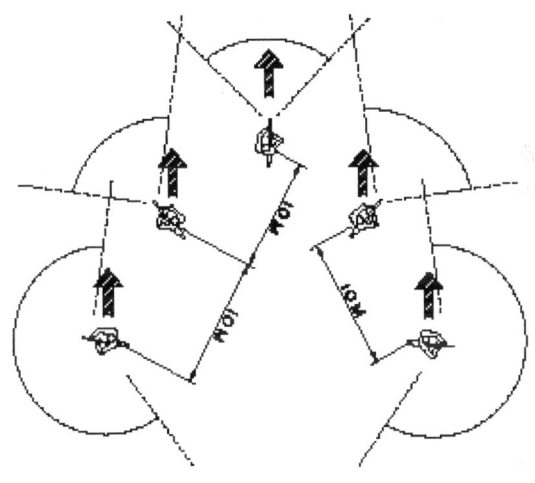

A typical wedge formation with sectors of fire shown.

     This is the most common US Army Infantry combat formation and is practiced at every opportunity. Get into your wedge formation and practice walking as a team through the woods.

Walking in a line towards the objective would be used to flush out opponents and employ all available firepower onto a target to the front.

Each team member should walk side by side with 10 to 20 feet between them and drop to the ground upon contact.

This formation provides 100% security to the front or rear with minimal cover to the sides.

This formation is easily spotted and flanked.

With this formations shortcomings also comes its versatility.   It enables the entire formation to put the maximum available firepower to the front towards the enemy and is the standard infantry and armored combat formation for most Warsaw Pact countries.

This formation is typically deployed with units side by side to form a wide 'front' and echeloned deep. If the first few echelons get destroyed or mowed down, the following echelons move through. In WWII the Russians typically would give weapons to only the first few echelons expecting the following echelons to pick up weapons from their fallen comrades. It is rumored that the modern N. Koreans and Chinese do the same.

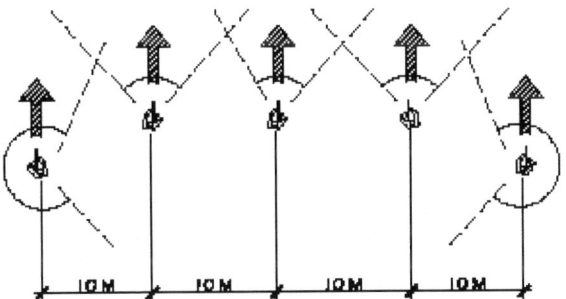

Staggered and Stack Formations are typically used where space is limited as in a building, down hallways or in large rooms.

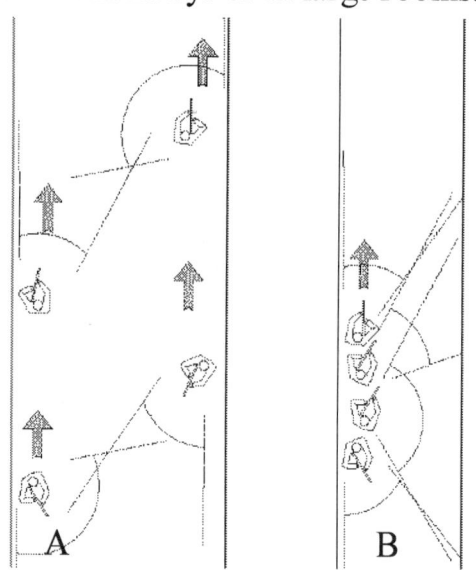

A. Staggered column in hallway showing sectors of fire.

B. Stack formation in hallway showing sectors of fire.

3.5 Security (Rooms or Small Spaces)

With each team member covering their respective sectors, the responsibility of the teams security is everyone's.

Cover openings, ensure that at least one team member has rear security. With the rest of the team covering uncleared openings. The only exception to this rule is when your team is storming into a room. The rule is get through the 'choke point' (doorway) as quickly as possible and immediately disperse.

    A team enters a room and disperses to clear it and immediately gets back into the stack formation, including rear security to storm the next room.   The uncleared doorway into the next space is watched by the person whose sector it falls into until the team regroups.

3.6 Security (open area)

Maintain security, high and low, front, rear and to the sides.

A team enters a large room and disperses as usual. Moving very quickly the team orients itself to the uncleared opening(s) and gets back into the stack formation to continue the assault on the building.

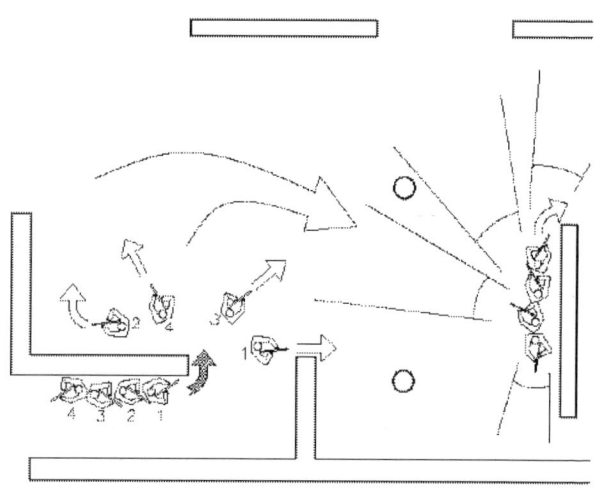

A team enters a large open space. Upon clearing it they do one of two things. Get into a hasty defensive posture or re-form to assault the next space, covering each opening and moving very quickly while in the stack formation. The entire team could be wiped out with one burst while in the stack formation. Assaulting and dispersing very quickly into the next space is critical.

3.7 Observation posts (OP)

An observation post could be used as a sniper team looking for enemy flanking units or to guard your flag.

Communications with your assaulting force is recommended. A two way radio or even your cell phone would work.

As an OP, your responsibility would be guarding your flag or reporting enemy movement. Having communications with your assaulting force would enable them to react to enemy assaults on your position. Your assaulting force could break contact with their enemy engagement to flank the opposing probing force into your base.

The OP should engage the opponent at a distance for suppression. This is called "Fixing" your opponent. You are temporarily fixing their position by hindering their ability to move.

Call your QRF or assaulting force back to flank them. If your assaulting force is already engaged with your opponent, they should break contact to reinforce your defense, by flanking the opposing assaulting force.

Considerations for the OP

Security
Communications

Your OP can be most effective if equipped with a two way radio. They could also lead an assaulting force into your kill zone by making contact, and falling back past your ambush without alerting them of your ambush location.

3.8   Quick Reaction Force (QRF)

A quick reaction force could be as small as a two to three person team.

The QRF could be effectively deployed as a hidden flanking force of an assault, to scout forward, to cut off the likely avenue of retreat and performing a hasty ambush, to reinforce your OP.   The options are limitless.   Radio contact with both the OP and Assaulting force would be perfect.

QRF Deployment suggestions:

Scout forward to find the opponent and withdraw and call your main assault group.

Flank the opponent or reinforce the main assault

Set up a hasty ambush behind a larger opposing force (undetected)

Set up an OP for observation / security to reinforce your flag group or assault group, whoever needs assistance.

A typical 10 person team

2 snipers / OP (guard)
2 person QRF
6 person Main assault group
   (divided into 2 teams)

-or-

3 person QRF
7 person Main assault group
(divided into 2 teams)

You get the idea.

Chapter 3 Notes

4. Reconnaissance / Stealth

Reconnoiter to locate the opposing team and familiarize yourself with the terrain. Knowledge of your surroundings enables you to formulate a solid plan and may mean victory for your team.

In a real world combat situation reconnaissance patrols are conducted to familiarize you with the lay of the land and to search for and locate possible enemy positions. The buildings, the obstacles, the covered routes that could be used by an attacking force all should be learned.

Often in game play, you will not have an opportunity to scout the land before the game starts.

4.1 Urban Recon

Your QRF (Quick Reaction Force) could be utilized as your R&S (reconnaissance and security) team. Scout ahead avoiding likely ambush sites and break contact with larger forces. They are scouting only, not assaulting and should break contact (withdraw under fire) if they encounter a larger force.

Once linked with the assaulting force and out of sight (and mind) of the opposition, they can begin to consider flanking maneuvers or simply reinforcing the main assault element.

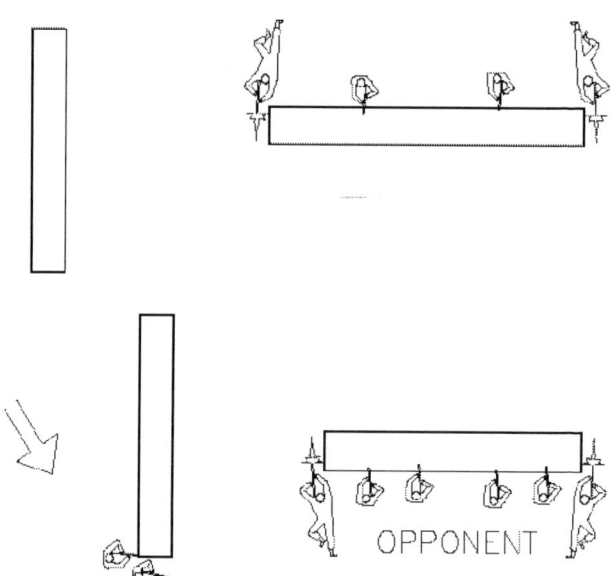

The two man recon team flanks the opposing force.

4.2 Indoor Urban Recon in Force

Recon in force is where you'd deploy your entire assault team as recon. For a small course, this may be your only option.

Send a small part of your team ahead to avoid ambushes (A point man or scout). This would give your assault element more options for maneuverability in the event of contact.

The main element is right behind the 'scout'. Distance from the enemy enables the main element more maneuverability options such as flanking. If your scout doesn't get himself knocked out of the game, you could reinforce him as a distraction force to hold his forward position and conduct your main assault from a flanking position.

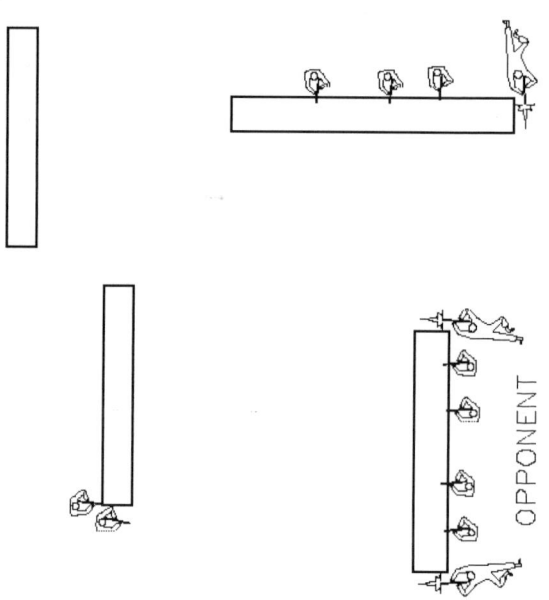

        The two man recon team locates and
fixes the opposing force while the main
assault element flanks the opposition.

4.3 Camouflage

Blend in with your surroundings. Urban camouflage, gray or black does this effectively, unless you are in a brightly lit and colorful indoor course.

Break up your outline, from your helmet, body, arms, legs to your boots. A snipers guillie suit does this effectively. Use the natural vegetation of your area or try to match it with man made materials like burlap strips.

Use camouflage face paint for your hands and face, or wear gloves and a full camouflaged face mask with the outline broken.

4.4 Light & Noise discipline

Do not leave shiny or light colored objects in view.   Paint shiny equipment to prevent detection.

Do not use a flashlight or other light source during night operations.   Navigate or scan using night vision devices, moon or starlight.   Your eyes will adjust to low light levels.

Do not speak unless necessary.   See chapter 9 for hand and arm signals for communication between team mates during silent operations.

Move silently while approaching an enemy position.

4.5 Moving with stealth

Moving with stealth means moving quietly, slowly and very carefully to avoid noise and detection.

Ensure solid footing by keeping all of your weight on the foot on the ground while stepping.

Raise your moving foot high to clear branches, brush or grasses.

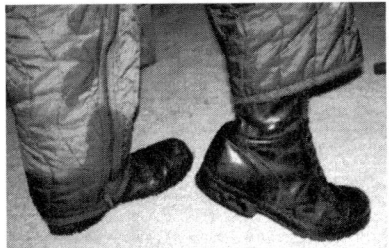

Gently let the moving foot down toe first, with your body's weight on your rear leg, careful to avoid twigs, loose stones and dead leaves.

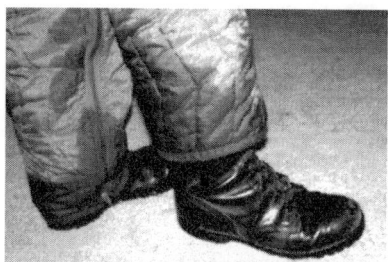

Lower the heel of your moving foot after the toe is in a solid place.

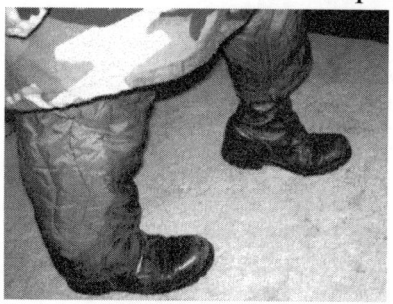

Shift your body's weight and balance to the forward foot before moving the rear foot.

Take short steps to maintain your balance.

Kneel down periodically behind cover to listen to the sounds of your environment and attempt to detect the presence of "enemy" contestants through their noisy and sloppy movements.

4.6 Scanning

There are two steps to proper and effective scanning.

First, make an overall search of the entire area for obvious targets, unnatural colors, shadows, outlines or movement. Do this first step quickly.

Second, the overlapping search side to side. Start close to you position and move outward scanning side to side. Search all suspicious spots well.

Chapter 4 Notes

5. Moving through the indoor playing field

Maneuvering yourself and your team to victory in what would be a high intensity and a high stress environment requires quick reflexes, skill in basic movement techniques, marksmanship and above all enough stamina to quickly and effectively eliminate all of your opposition.

Practice these techniques all day every day for a week and you'd scratch the surface of what our infantrymen do and have done everyday, with 100 lbs of gear for a typical deployment overseas.

Practice makes perfect, but even if you train constantly and continually a novice could easily take you out.

Here are some techniques that with practice, may keep your team on top.

5.1 Combat patrol

A combat patrol is basically a recon and security patrol. Locate your opponent to harass or destroy them.

The two types of a combat patrol are the ambush and raid.

Raids are conducted to harass or assault your opponent.

An ambush is a surprise attack.

See chapter 7 for Ambush

5.2 Crossing danger areas (moving between barriers, passing doors, etc.)

While moving past a danger area (open door, hallway, etc.) post a security element covering the danger area to move your team across.   Normally this would be your first man in the 4 man stack.

Security is the most important factor in safely moving your team.

The security element could easily be reinforced if you make contact with your opponent.

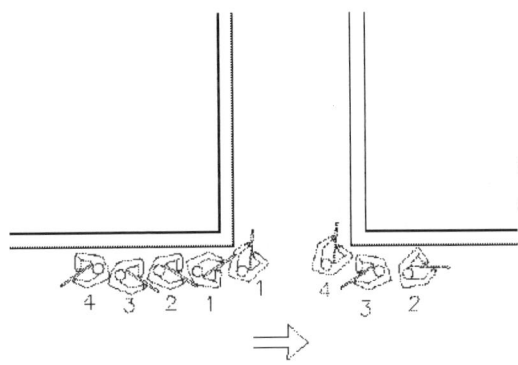

After you pass the danger area, the first person security element takes up rear security. Your entire team should almost leap-frog through a building providing security at each possible danger area.

The second man obviously then becomes the first person in the stack. Each person will conduct operations acting in each position in the stack if properly executed. Four people working as a perfect team.

5.3 bound by buddy teams

One two person team moves while the other team provides security and / or suppressive fire.

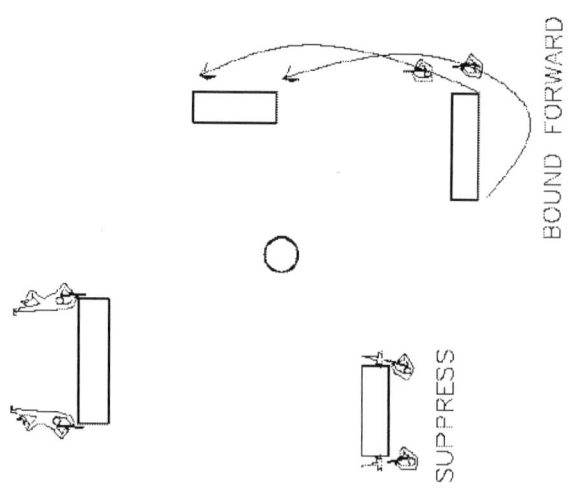

5.4 turning corners (pie)

Slowly turn corners revealing one 'slice' at a time. You are visually clearing each portion of the field, hall or room as you slowly turn a corner.

Do not stick the end of your weapon out past the corner. If there were opposing team members there, they will see it and will be prepared when you come around the corner.

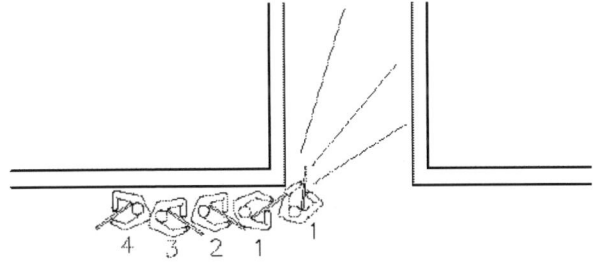

Each line down the hall from person #1 in the above illustration is a piece of the hallway that is revealed as it is visually cleared.

5.5 Entering a room individually.

Upon approaching a door, and moving into the room becomes necessary, quickly peek into the room, then rush in staying close to the wall in which you approached the door way. As you move into the room you quickly scan the entire room.

Let's assume you are moving through a corridor and a door is to your left. Move up to the door while moving silently; peek in to visually clear the center of the room (pie). Rush in, stay close to the wall on your left side, and quickly swing to clear the Right, center and finally the left corner. Keeping your weapon 'at the ready' will allow you to quickly defeat your opponent.

One thing to consider. As you approach the door, begin to formulate your plan for entering. You do not want to pause

5.6. Entering a room as part of a team

Get your team into a four person stack formation, with all weapons at the ready position quickly and without any unnecessary pauses in your teams' assault momentum just outside the door or the room you want to assault.

Always enter a room following the path of least resistance. Get your entire team into the room and away from the door as quickly as possible. The door is a choke point, moving slowly and unorganized, your entire team could be wiped out by one defender.

Example Assaulting from left side of door (left shoulder against corridor wall)

The first person goes through, crosses the door and sticks to the opposite (right) wall and moves to the right corner, then turns to clear along the wall towards the far corner.

The first person initially goes in the direction of where he / she thinks that the greatest threat may be, otherwise he would be exposing his back to a known opponent.

As the first person enters the second person is immediately behind and sticks to the opposite wall, moves around the door frame to clear the left corner, then turns to clear along the wall towards the far corner.

Immediately following the second person comes the third rushing in, the third person breaks off and clears the center of the room on the left or right side, whichever is easier.

The trail or Fourth person immediately comes in and clears the opposite side of that the third person covered.

The entire team enters the room almost at the same time and covers their respective sectors. This should happen for a four man team in 1.5 seconds or less to overwhelm your opponent.

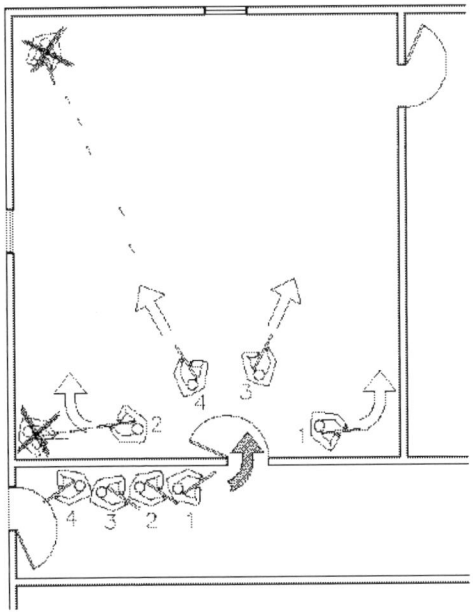

Note: If any person in your team gets hit while moving through the doorway, someone else has to secure that area and knock out the threat. The person immediately behind the person that got hit may not be facing that way. Your primary concern is killing a threat in front of you, then someone else. Be prepared to think and react quickly to a bad situation. Make sure you get out of the choke point.

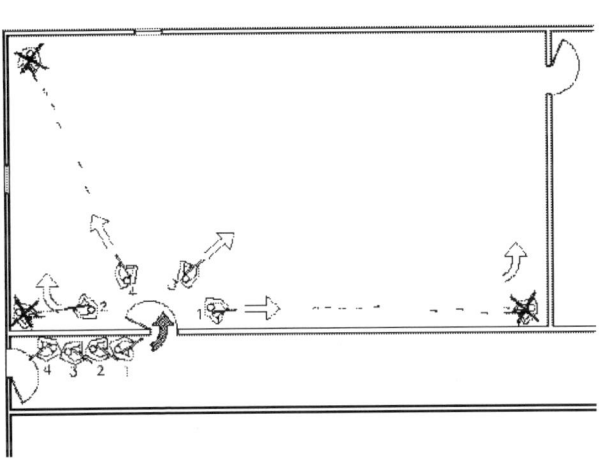

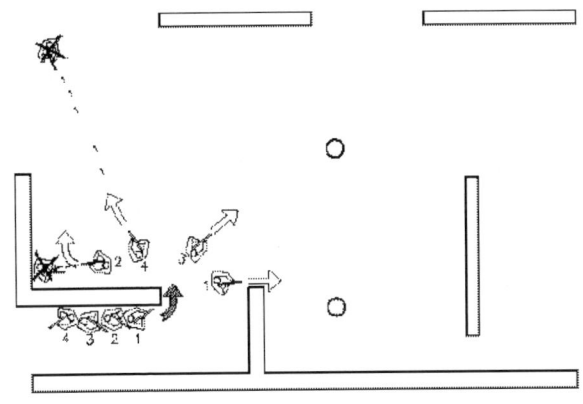

5.7 Crossing a wall

If you must cross a wall to flank or outmaneuver your opponent, ensure that you minimize your exposure. Find a low spot to visually check the opposite side for obstacles or the opponent. Quickly roll over the top of the wall. Always cross a wall rapidly minimizing your exposure and profile. Keep your opponent from getting an easy shot at you.

Once the first person has crossed, provide security for your remaining team members to cross after you.

5.8 Hallway movement

If you need to move down a hallway stay close to the walls to minimize your target profile. Quickly move down the hallway, re-form into your stack and quickly assault the next room.

Attempt to surprise any occupant in the room by keeping your team's noise to a minimum and reacting to rooms with swift and violent action. Do not lose your momentum.

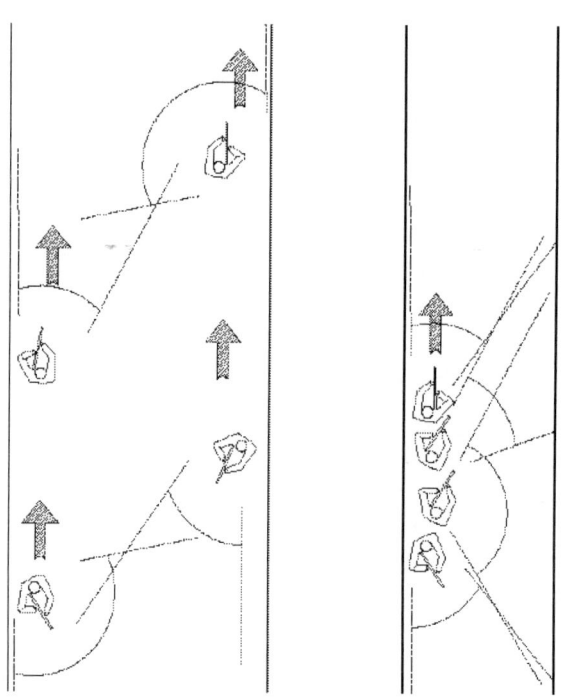

For a wide hallway, a staggered formation is recommended. Quickly get into the stack formation immediately before assaulting a room or space.

Chapter 5 Notes

6. Contact

6.1 Firing around an obstacle

Firing around the side of an obstacle or an object that provides you with cover and concealment is the preferred method of engagement.

You can quickly peek around a corner or obstacle to see where your opponent is.

Preferably you'd get into the prone firing position to minimize your profile, but quite often you will need to maneuver and unless you're defending, the prone position wouldn't be practical.

Kneeling and firing around an obstacle would offer the reduced profile and the maneuverability that will keep you in the game.

6.2 Firing above an Obstacle

See chapter 8.3 Defending your Bunker.

It is recommended to fire around an obstacle as opposed to over it because bullets and paint balls ricochet.

You also have a few inches at the top of your head that is visible by your opponent before you can actually see anything down the course.

Firing above an obstacle is not recommended unless you are out of options.

6.3 Team Firing Positions

Moving as a team, coming into contact, you do not want to bunch up and have two or more people out of the game from one volley from your opponent, but you do want to get as many of your team members firing at your target as possible.

Maneuver to deploy your team so that each member has a good field of fire for suppression and can also provide security. While you are engaging your opponent, you may have another opposing player attempting to flank or come in behind you.

Military machine gunners employ a tactic called talking guns. One fires a burst, pauses and the other machine gun fires. Count to three, pause for three, etc.

6.4 Suppression

Talking guns is the preferred method for suppressing your opponent. One team fires then pauses, the other team fires.

You are trying to keep them from moving and to keep their heads down while your team maneuvers. It's much easier to change your position and maneuver when no one is shooting at you. That is why you would want to fire enough to keep their heads down without giving them an opportunity to move or to return fire.

6.5 Crossfire

Maneuvering your team with a flanking element to pin down your opponent and eliminate them from play is easiest when you can maneuver to obtain perfect cross fire.   You are effectively eliminating anything that they could hide behind.

If you or your team find yourself in crossfire, you have two options. Assault or withdraw.

You would want to assault if they are close, within 20 feet and withdraw if you cannot effectively assault in one short charge.

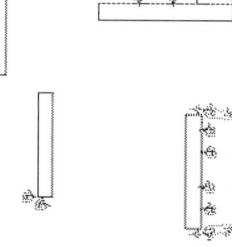

6.6 Withdraw under fire

Getting caught in the crossfire or facing a numerically superior force, you would want to withdraw under fire. Attempt to suppress your opponent while scanning for a position to fall back to. It might be best to quickly turn around and return to the position you just left.

Ideally you would have another team to provide suppression to cover your withdrawal.

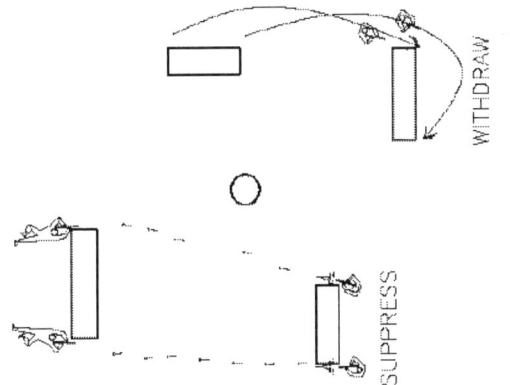

6.7 Defending to the Last Man

See 8.2 defending a room

As the last man on your team, you would want to consider employing guerrilla tactics.   Opportunistic attack and withdraw.

Set up a hasty ambush in a room, if you hear movement coming your way; spray a volley of shots towards your opponent. Immediately withdraw before they can react and return fire.

Fall back into at least one space behind your current position, trying not to get flanked or suppressed (pinned down).

Let them come to you.   Wait for them to assault the room you were in, then spray through the door towards their position, and again fall back.

Keep moving to keep them on their toes. When the opportunity arises spray a volley of shots into them, but immediately fall back before they return fire.

Don't fall back far enough where you lose track of where they are and be sure to let them think that they know where you are. Do not get cornered.

Try to avoid a firefight by falling back and employing multiple hasty ambushes. Surprise is your advantage.

Chapter 6 notes

7. Ambush

Ambushes make up one of two types of combat patrols. The first is a raid (assault), second, an ambush.

There are two categories of ambushes, Deliberate and Hasty.

There are also two types of ambushes, point or area

Finally there is the formation employed in the ambush. Lineal or 'L' shaped, or any modification of the two based on time or terrain. There are a million ways to properly execute an ambush and often time available or terrain will dictate how your team is laid out, dug in a set up. Be prepared to modify your plan according to the situation.

The element of surprise is the critical element of any category or type of ambush. Setting up an ambush in an urban environment is not as hard as it may seem. There are many factors in your favor. Cover and concealment is usually abundant. The real key to success is to select an ambush site that severely limits your opponent's ability to maneuver out of your kill zone or find and hide behind cover.

Set your people in a concealed defensive position and hold your fire until your opponents are in your kill zone.

The priority of fires would be their leading, trailing and especially flanking elements.

Wait until they are close to your position without detecting you. Close proximity will limit their ability to maneuver, but also limits their options.   They can perform a close assault, or panic and run.

Ideally, they would be stuck in your kill zone and wiped out.

7.1 Deliberate Ambush

A deliberate ambush is planned and prepared along a known or obvious route.

7.2 Hasty Ambush

A hasty ambush is performed when you see your opponent before they see you. You have time to get into a defensive position undetected and utilize the element of surprise.

7.3 Point Ambush

A point ambush attempts to isolate and pin down (fix) and destroy your opponent in a single kill zone.

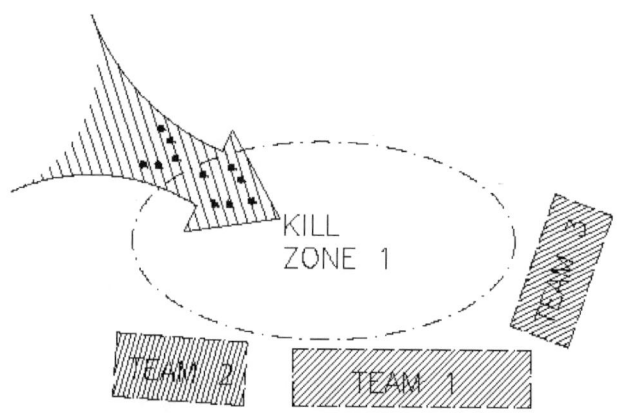

Note: Possible escape routes are not covered.

7.4 Area Ambush

An area ambush deploys your team into two or more, smaller ambush sites.

Normally by U.S. military doctrine, an infantry platoon of 30 plus soldiers would be the smallest unit making up one of the parts of an area ambush.   For paintball, two man teams would work.

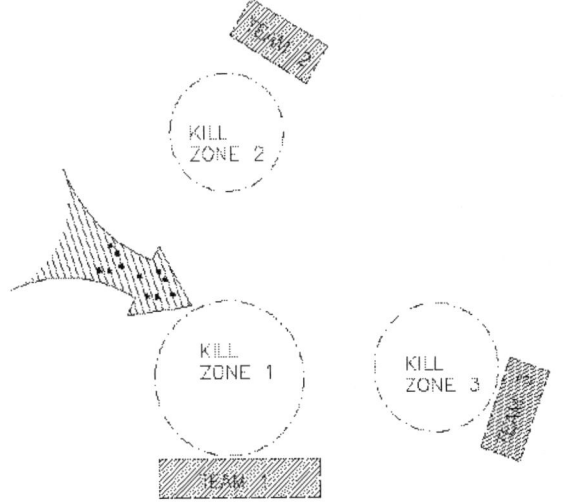

Kill zone 1 is the primary ambush site.

Kill zones 2 and 3 are possible enemy escape routes. The teams in kill zones 2 and 3 stay in their concealed positions while the enemy passes through their kill zone.

The main ambush begins in kill zone 1. If the ambush is prematurely sprung by the teams in kill zone 2 or 3, the entire ambush becomes ineffective.

It would be recommended to put only experienced people in teams 2 and 3.

7.5 Linear Ambush

In a linear ambush your team would select covered and concealed firing positions along the known or expected route that your opponent will move through.

After initiating the ambush and the opponents are either pinned or are falling back, your entire team would assault across the kill zone, bounding by buddy teams.

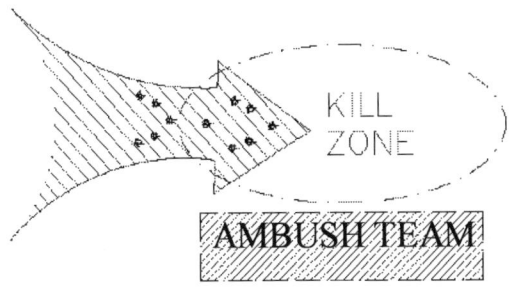

7.6 'L' shaped Ambush

In an L shaped ambush your team would select covered and concealed firing positions along the known or expected route of travel by your opponent with an assaulting leg.

The short leg of the 'L' would be the assault element. After the ambush has been sprung and the remaining members of the opposing team are pinned down or are falling back, the assault element moves across the kill zone. This effectively puts your opponent in your cross fire and eliminates anything that they can effectively hide behind.

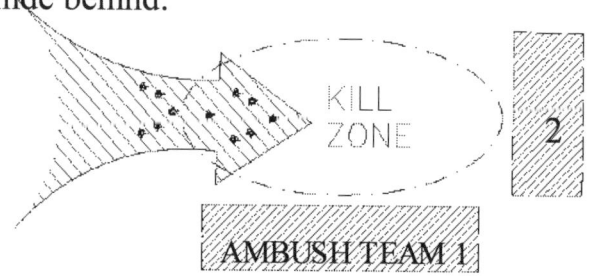

Chapter 7 Notes

8. Fighting / Defensive Positions

8.1 Hasty fighting position

Fight wherever you come in contact using whatever fighting posture you deem most suited for your quickest response to the threat.

8.2 Defending a room

As the defender of a room if someone or the entire opposing team unexpectedly enters and moves quickly across the room, it will take a second of two for you to get a bead on them and fire. This natural lag in response could be used against you if you are facing a team who has trained using these or similar techniques.

An organized team who has trained to properly clear a room will leave no area of the room unsearched within the first two seconds. They will be moving quickly to eliminate any threat.

No matter how prepared you are, a disciplined team running in to your room will usually take you out, especially if they move silently and give you no indication that they are about to storm the room. Your best defense is to select a position in the room behind cover.   If no cover is available, stick to one of the walls by the door.   Lying down also helps because they are usually scanning at about waist height.

  Select a wall opposite the door that enables you a clear shot to each door.   If you are defending a room with someone else,   ensure that neither one of you will get in the way of each other.   Try to avoid getting your opponent between you.   Avoid friendly kills, fratricide.

8.3 Defending your bunker

Try to utilize windows or small holes (firing ports or 'loopholes') in the walls.

Avoid firing over the walls.   Position yourself at a door or other vertical opening. Construct your bunker with a crenulated wall, similar to a castle wall.   Build multiple small firing ports and larger solid pieces of wall so that you have cover, some concealment and a few options.   If everyone is concentrating on one opening, would it make sense to show your smiling face?

You should not fire more than 3 bursts from any one opening.   Switch firing ports after every few shots to keep them guessing where you'll show up next.

8.4 Moving Defense (Ambush and withdraw)

You could surprise the opposing assaulting team by firing at them down a hallway and then falling back into a room. You'd be letting them know that you are there, but a quick hasty ambush to knock out one or two before they get to you would make the defense a lot easier.

Fall back or move but try not to get yourself surrounded or pinned down. Attempt to stay one room behind them. After they clear the room you just left conduct a hasty ambush into the room they just cleared.   Fire a 2 second burst to cover the room of greatest threat and fall back again.

Chapter 8 Notes

9. Infantry Hand and Arm signals

Seeing a hand and arm signal you should make eye contact with the person behind you and repeat the hand and arm signal so that everyone knows what is going on. (These hand and arm signals build confidence and cohesion in moving silently as a group and also reinforces the effectiveness in the use of these hand and arm signals). Be open to make up and improvise new or different hand and arm signals. Go over each of them so that everyone knows what each of them mean.

During the actual engagement, yell to be heard. Silence is no longer necessary.

As soon as the threat is destroyed, immediately return to stealth. Moving and communicating quickly and silently.

This list has been taken from
'Handbook of Infantry tactics
for Paint-ball'
© 2009 D. Wagner

* Are you ready- palm out, arm extended

* Assign a Sector – Chopping motion to
each side of you bending at the elbow at 45
degrees to your left and right, or what ever
sector you want covered.

* Bounding over watch, (by squad) –
Similar to Bound by teams but with flat
hand. symbolizing one squad moves while
the other squad covers.   Flat hand, then roll
your arms like you're pedaling.

* Bound by teams – two fingers up with
one hand, then rolling your arms, like
pedaling.

* Cover me – Finger extended up with palm
of other hand over it.

* **Danger area ahead** – Open palm down, slash across your chest diagonally.

* **Double time (RUN)** – Pump arm over your head

* **Enemy in sight** – hand extended like an upside down pistol

* **Flank Left** – Extend left arm out like a one arm hug, while extending finger pointing in direction of travel.

* **Flank Right** - Extend right arm out like a one arm hug, while extending finger pointing in direction of travel.

* **Follow me** – With your arm extended behind you with your palms up and open, bring your arm over your head in a wide arc.

Formations

* **Diamond formation** – Put your hands together to form a diamond.

* **File Formation** – Chopping motion behind you.

* **Line formation** – Both Arms out to your side in a chopping motion, if you are in the middle, otherwise one arm in the direction you want everyone to go.

* **Staggered File Formation** – Chopping motion staggered, chop to one side then the other like making an 'x' (while moving).

* **Wedge Formation** – Two fingers extended horizontal, similar to peace sign with palm facing downward.

* **Group together** – With your hands open, motion like you're pushing two objects together.

* **Halt** – Fist above your head.

* **Head count** – Pat the top of your head, Each man quietly counts to let the leader know how many people are available, or if anyone got left behind.

* **Leader, 1 Sqd** – Shake your collar and hold up 1 finger.

* **Leader, 2 Sqd** – Shake your collar and hold up 2 fingers.

* **Move in that direction** – point in direction of travel.

* **Move with stealth** – Slow walking fingers over open hand.

* **Quiet** – One finger to your lips.

* **Rally Point** – Rotate hand over head then point to an area designated to fall back to.

* **Scan your sector** – Point to eyes then out, side to side.

* **Scroll the road** – Tap your shoulder then roll one hand down your arm.

* **Security** – Point to your eyes with two fingers from one hand.

* **Traveling Security/Scout to the front** – Point to your eyes with two fingers on one hand, Then Put your hands together then open them moving away from you towards the direction of travel. Chop with far hand. Point to direction of travel.

* Traveling Security/Scout to the side – Point to your eyes with one hand, Then Put your hands together opening them to the side away from you in the direction you want to post security. Slide hand (back to front) with far hand to your side, Chop and point to direction of travel.

* Spread out – With the backs of your hands together, open them like you're pushing two objects apart.

* Team 1 – One finger raised.

* Team 2 – Two fingers raised.

* Withdraw – Backward chop while extending one finger towards direction to move to.

Hand and arm signals should be adapted or modified to your team. Discuss what signals your team should add modify or use. Ensure that every member of your team is aware of what each one means and what actions they should take when they see it.

The lack of illustrations enables each team to communicate the same thing differently. Enabling a silent 'code' understood only by your team.

Chapter 9 Notes

10. Military unit map symbols

These symbols are used to identify unit type, location, and command size and unit name if known.

Typically, the only symbols you might use in gaming would be Infantry, Scouts etc. If you have a tank in your yard, maybe Armor symbols.

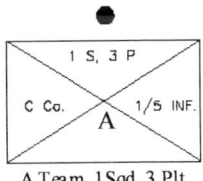

A Team, 1 Sqd, 3 Plt

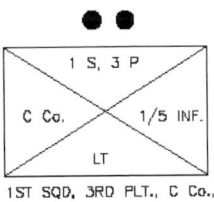

1ST SQD, 3RD PLT., C Co., 1/5 INF REG., 2 ID

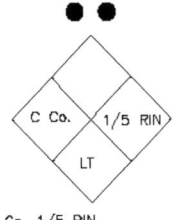

C Co. 1/5 RIN
1/5 INF REG.(LT, LIGHT INFANTRY), 2 ID
(ENEMY)

Basic Unit identification map symbols to be used on top of the unit identification marker

i   Individual

ii   Buddy team

iii or *   Fire team

*   Fire team

**   Squad

***   Platoon

I	Company
II	Battalion
III	Regiment
X	Brigade
XX	Division
XXX	Corps
XXXX	Army Group

All you would use for planning a small war game might be the fire team, squad and maybe platoon.

Company size and above unit size identifiers are provided for information only. They could be used if you had a few hundred thousand people on your team...

Here are a few useful symbols.
There is no need to show airborne, artillery
or any other symbol that couldn't possibly
be used in paint-ball. Mech. and Armor are
included for fun.   For enemy symbols, use a
diamond shape as illustrated at the
beginning of this chapter.

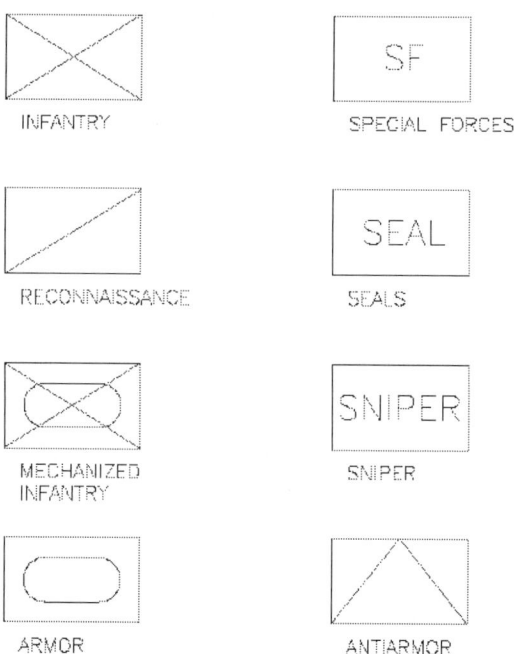

INFANTRY

SPECIAL FORCES

RECONNAISSANCE

SEALS

MECHANIZED
INFANTRY

SNIPER

ARMOR

ANTIARMOR

Use these symbols for your area or your indoor course.

You should be able to find a web-site that shows the geographical information for your area. Print it out, put your unit symbols on and have fun planning your next battle.

For your indoor course, simply sketch the layout and arrange your team or plan your defense.

Chapter 10 Notes

Glossary of terms
AA: Avenue of Approach

AO: Area of Operations

ASL: Assistant Squad Leader

Ambush: A surprise attack on the enemy
as they pass through an area.

Avenue of approach: The most likely
route that the enemy will approach from.

Bound(ing):   Moving as a buddy team, fire
team or squad where ½ of the element
moves while the other ½ is in position and
covers your movement by scanning for or
suppressing the enemy.

Combat operations: Any part of planning,
moving, preparing for or engaging the
enemy.

Communications (Commo): Radio, phone, voice, hand and arm signals

Concealment: Anything that you can hide behind that obscures sight but does not block shots.

Cover: Anything that you can hide behind that blocks shots.

CP: Command Post

Doctrine: Rules established by your government or unit.

Engagement: Firing at the enemy, locked in combat.

Fire team: 3-6 people or soldiers operating as a team.

Flank: Attack from the side or rear of the enemy element.

Formation: The arrangement of people or vehicles

Hasty: Quick unprepared position.

Heavy Infantry: Mechanized Infantry. Infantry that has vehicles attached to their unit.

In Force: All available men and equipment.

Light Infantry: Soldiers whose primary job is to fight on foot, without the benefit of or support from vehicles.

Maneuver: Any skillful movement or shift in orientation.

Marksmanship: The ability to hit what you're aiming for, utilizing the fundamentals of shooting.

MOUT: Military Operations in Urban Terrain, Fighting in or around any arrangement of buildings.

Objective: Any place where the enemy combatant(s) are set up to defend or a key piece of terrain.

Obstacles: Any thing that blocks or hinders movement or sight through an area.

OP : Observation Post: Placed in front of to the side of the main element to observe enemy movement.

Over watch: Security, scanning for the enemy, while a team moves.

PDF: Principle Direction of Fire

Point: Lead scout.

Pursuit: Chasing the enemy.

Raid: One type of combat patrol.   Attack and withdraw.

Reconnaissance: Obtaining information of military value regarding terrain, location, strength and movement of enemy forces.

Sector of fire: The areas that you are responsible for scanning for the enemy.

Security: Eyes on 360 degrees of your perimeter or danger areas, to include front, flanks and rear security.

Sight picture: The alignment of your front and rear sights, or the sight through your scope.

SOP: Standard operating procedure

Suppressive fire: Firing just enough to keep the enemy's heads down without an opportunity for them to return fire or observe your movements.

SWAT: Special Weapons And Tactics

TRP: Target Reference Point

Zero: Adjustment of your sights so that your rounds or paintballs hit what you're aiming for.   It may be necessary to elevate your sight picture for further shots taking into account the drop of your paint balls over a distance as long as the rounds land straight onto what you're aiming for without sideway movement.

References:
STP 21-1-SMCT Warrior Skills Level 1,
Dec. 2007,
Approved for public release

FM 7-8 Infantry Rifle Platoon and Squad,
April 1992,
Approved for public release

Notes:

Notes:

2679710

Made in the USA